THIS PLANNER BELONGS TO:

_____

CONTACTS

NAME	ADDRESS	NUMBERS

2021

JANUARY

SUN	MON	TUE	WED	THU	FRI	SAT
					1	2
3	4	5	6	7	8	9
10	11	12	13	14	15	16
17	18	19	20	21	22	23
24	25	26	27	28	29	30
31						

FEBRUARY

SUN	MON	TUE	WED	THU	FRI	SAT
	1	2	3	4	5	6
7	8	9	10	11	12	13
14	15	16	17	18	19	20
21	22	23	24	25	26	27
28						

MARCH

SUN	MON	TUE	WED	THU	FRI	SAT
	1	2	3	4	5	6
7	8	9	10	11	12	13
14	15	16	17	18	19	20
21	22	23	24	25	26	27
28	29	30	31			

APRIL

SUN	MON	TUE	WED	THU	FRI	SAT
				1	2	3
4	5	6	7	8	9	10
11	12	13	14	15	16	17
18	19	20	21	22	23	24
25	26	27	28	29	30	

MAY

SUN	MON	TUE	WED	THU	FRI	SAT
						1
2	3	4	5	6	7	8
9	10	11	12	13	14	15
16	17	18	19	20	21	22
23	24	25	26	27	28	29
30	31					

JUNE

SUN	MON	TUE	WED	THU	FRI	SAT
		1	2	3	4	5
6	7	8	9	10	11	12
13	14	15	16	17	18	19
20	21	22	23	24	25	26
27	28	29	30			

JULY

SUN	MON	TUE	WED	THU	FRI	SAT
				1	2	3
4	5	6	7	8	9	10
11	12	13	14	15	16	17
18	19	20	21	22	23	24
25	26	27	28	29	30	31

AUGUST

SUN	MON	TUE	WED	THU	FRI	SAT
1	2	3	4	5	6	7
8	9	10	11	12	13	14
15	16	17	18	19	20	21
22	23	24	25	26	27	28
29	30	31				

SEPTEMBER

SUN	MON	TUE	WED	THU	FRI	SAT
			1	2	3	4
5	6	7	8	9	10	11
12	13	14	15	16	17	18
19	20	21	22	23	24	25
26	27	28	29	30		

OCTOBER

SUN	MON	TUE	WED	THU	FRI	SAT
					1	2
3	4	5	6	7	8	9
10	11	12	13	14	15	16
17	18	19	20	21	22	23
24	25	26	27	28	29	30
31						

NOVEMBER

SUN	MON	TUE	WED	THU	FRI	SAT
	1	2	3	4	5	6
7	8	9	10	11	12	13
14	15	16	17	18	19	20
21	22	23	24	25	26	27
28	29	30				

DECEMBER

SUN	MON	TUE	WED	THU	FRI	SAT
			1	2	3	4
5	6	7	8	9	10	11
12	13	14	15	16	17	18
19	20	21	22	23	24	25
26	27	28	29	30	31	

IMPORTANT DATES

July 2021

SUNDAY	MONDAY	TUESDAY	WEDNESDAY
4 Independence Day	**5**	**6**	**7**
11	**12**	**13**	**14**
18	**19**	**20**	**21**
25	**26**	**27**	**28**

A person who never made a mistake never tried anything new.

– Albert Einstein

THURSDAY	FRIDAY	SATURDAY	NOTES
1	2	3	
8	9	10	
15	16	17	
22	23	24	
29	30	31	

June 2021

28 MONDAY

☐
☐
☐
☐
☐
☐
☐
☐
☐
☐

29 TUESDAY

☐
☐
☐
☐
☐
☐
☐
☐
☐
☐
☐

30 WEDNESDAY

☐
☐
☐
☐
☐
☐
☐
☐
☐
☐
☐

July 2021

1 THURSDAY

☐
☐
☐
☐
☐
☐
☐
☐
☐
☐
☐

2 FRIDAY

☐
☐
☐
☐
☐
☐
☐
☐
☐
☐
☐

3 SATURDAY

4 SUNDAY

Independence Day

July 2021

5 **MONDAY**

☐
☐
☐
☐
☐
☐
☐
☐
☐
☐
☐

6 **TUESDAY**

☐
☐
☐
☐
☐
☐
☐
☐
☐
☐
☐

7 **WEDNESDAY**

☐
☐
☐
☐
☐
☐
☐
☐
☐
☐
☐
☐

8 THURSDAY

☐
☐
☐
☐
☐
☐
☐
☐
☐
☐
☐

9 FRIDAY

☐
☐
☐
☐
☐
☐
☐
☐
☐
☐
☐

10 SATURDAY

11 SUNDAY

July 2021

12 **MONDAY**

☐
☐
☐
☐
☐
☐
☐
☐
☐
☐
☐

13 **TUESDAY**

☐
☐
☐
☐
☐
☐
☐
☐
☐
☐
☐

14 **WEDNESDAY**

☐
☐
☐
☐
☐
☐
☐
☐
☐
☐
☐

15 THURSDAY

☐
☐
☐
☐
☐
☐
☐
☐
☐
☐
☐

16 FRIDAY

☐
☐
☐
☐
☐
☐
☐
☐
☐
☐
☐

17 SATURDAY

18 SUNDAY

July 2021

19 MONDAY

20 TUESDAY

21 WEDNESDAY

July 2021

22 THURSDAY

☐
☐
☐
☐
☐
☐
☐
☐
☐
☐
☐

23 FRIDAY

☐
☐
☐
☐
☐
☐
☐
☐
☐
☐
☐

24 SATURDAY

25 SUNDAY

July 2021

26 MONDAY

☐

☐

☐

☐

☐

☐

☐

☐

☐

☐

27 TUESDAY

☐

☐

☐

☐

☐

☐

☐

☐

☐

☐

28 WEDNESDAY

☐

☐

☐

☐

☐

☐

☐

☐

☐

☐

☐

☐

29 THURSDAY

☐
☐
☐
☐
☐
☐
☐
☐
☐
☐
☐

30 FRIDAY

☐
☐
☐
☐
☐
☐
☐
☐
☐
☐
☐

31 SATURDAY

1 SUNDAY

August 2021

SUNDAY	MONDAY	TUESDAY	WEDNESDAY
1	2	3	4
8	9	10	11
15	16	17	18
22	23	24	25
29	30	31	

I attribute my success to this: I never gave or took any excuse.

– Florence Nightingale

THURSDAY	FRIDAY	SATURDAY	NOTES
5	6	7	
12	13	14	
19	20	21	
26	27	28	

August 2021

2 MONDAY

☐
☐
☐
☐
☐
☐
☐
☐
☐
☐
☐

3 TUESDAY

☐
☐
☐
☐
☐
☐
☐
☐
☐
☐
☐

4 WEDNESDAY

☐
☐
☐
☐
☐
☐
☐
☐
☐
☐
☐
☐

5 **THURSDAY**

☐
☐
☐
☐
☐
☐
☐
☐
☐
☐
☐

6 **FRIDAY**

☐
☐
☐
☐
☐
☐
☐
☐
☐
☐
☐

7 **SATURDAY**

8 **SUNDAY**

August 2021

9 **MONDAY**

☐
☐
☐
☐
☐
☐
☐
☐
☐
☐

10 **TUESDAY**

☐
☐
☐
☐
☐
☐
☐
☐
☐
☐

11 **WEDNESDAY**

☐
☐
☐
☐
☐
☐
☐
☐
☐
☐
☐

12 THURSDAY

☐
☐
☐
☐
☐
☐
☐
☐
☐
☐
☐

13 FRIDAY

☐
☐
☐
☐
☐
☐
☐
☐
☐
☐
☐

14 SATURDAY

15 SUNDAY

August 2021

16 MONDAY

☐
☐
☐
☐
☐
☐
☐
☐
☐
☐
☐

17 TUESDAY

☐
☐
☐
☐
☐
☐
☐
☐
☐
☐
☐

18 WEDNESDAY

☐
☐
☐
☐
☐
☐
☐
☐
☐
☐
☐

19 THURSDAY

☐
☐
☐
☐
☐
☐
☐
☐
☐
☐
☐

20 FRIDAY

☐
☐
☐
☐
☐
☐
☐
☐
☐
☐
☐
☐

21 SATURDAY

22 SUNDAY

August 2021

23 MONDAY

24 TUESDAY

25 WEDNESDAY

26 THURSDAY

- [ ]
- [ ]
- [ ]
- [ ]
- [ ]
- [ ]
- [ ]
- [ ]
- [ ]
- [ ]
- [ ]

27 FRIDAY

- [ ]
- [ ]
- [ ]
- [ ]
- [ ]
- [ ]
- [ ]
- [ ]
- [ ]
- [ ]
- [ ]

28 SATURDAY

29 SUNDAY

September 2021

SUNDAY	MONDAY	TUESDAY	WEDNESDAY
			1
5	**6** Labor Day Rosh Hashanah, Begins at Sunset	**7**	**8**
12 Grandparents Day	**13**	**14**	**15** Yom Kippur, Begins at Sunset
19	**20**	**21**	**22** First Day of Autumn
26	**27**	**28**	**29**

The inner fire is the most important thing mankind possesses.

– Edith Södergran

THURSDAY	FRIDAY	SATURDAY	NOTES
2	**3**	**4**	
9	**10**	**11** Patriot Day	
16	**17**	**18**	
23	**24**	**25**	
30			

August 2021

30 MONDAY

_____
_____
_____
_____
_____
_____
_____
_____
_____
_____

☐
☐
☐
☐
☐
☐
☐
☐
☐
☐
☐

31 TUESDAY

_____
_____
_____
_____
_____
_____
_____
_____
_____
_____

☐
☐
☐
☐
☐
☐
☐
☐
☐
☐
☐

1 WEDNESDAY

_____
_____
_____
_____
_____
_____
_____
_____
_____

☐
☐
☐
☐
☐
☐
☐
☐
☐
☐
☐

September 2021

2 **THURSDAY**

- [ ]
- [ ]
- [ ]
- [ ]
- [ ]
- [ ]
- [ ]
- [ ]
- [ ]
- [ ]
- [ ]

3 **FRIDAY**

- [ ]
- [ ]
- [ ]
- [ ]
- [ ]
- [ ]
- [ ]
- [ ]
- [ ]
- [ ]
- [ ]

4 **SATURDAY**

5 **SUNDAY**

September 2021

6 MONDAY

Labor Day

Rosh Hashanah, Begins at Sunset

☐
☐
☐
☐
☐
☐
☐
☐
☐
☐
☐

7 TUESDAY

☐
☐
☐
☐
☐
☐
☐
☐
☐
☐
☐

8 WEDNESDAY

☐
☐
☐
☐
☐
☐
☐
☐
☐
☐
☐

9 **THURSDAY**

☐
☐
☐
☐
☐
☐
☐
☐
☐
☐
☐

10 **FRIDAY**

☐
☐
☐
☐
☐
☐
☐
☐
☐
☐
☐

11 **SATURDAY**

Patriot Day

12 **SUNDAY**

Grandparents Day

September 2021

13 MONDAY

☐
☐
☐
☐
☐
☐
☐
☐
☐
☐
☐

14 TUESDAY

☐
☐
☐
☐
☐
☐
☐
☐
☐
☐
☐

15 WEDNESDAY

Yom Kippur, Begins at Sunset

☐
☐
☐
☐
☐
☐
☐
☐
☐
☐
☐

16 THURSDAY

☐
☐
☐
☐
☐
☐
☐
☐
☐
☐
☐

17 FRIDAY

☐
☐
☐
☐
☐
☐
☐
☐
☐
☐
☐

18 SATURDAY

19 SUNDAY

September 2021

20 MONDAY

☐
☐
☐
☐
☐
☐
☐
☐
☐
☐
☐

21 TUESDAY

☐
☐
☐
☐
☐
☐
☐
☐
☐
☐
☐

22 WEDNESDAY

First Day of Autumn

☐
☐
☐
☐
☐
☐
☐
☐
☐
☐
☐

23 THURSDAY

☐
☐
☐
☐
☐
☐
☐
☐
☐
☐
☐

24 FRIDAY

☐
☐
☐
☐
☐
☐
☐
☐
☐
☐
☐

25 SATURDAY

26 SUNDAY

September 2021

27 MONDAY

_____ ☐ _____
_____ ☐ _____
_____ ☐ _____
_____ ☐ _____
_____ ☐ _____
_____ ☐ _____
_____ ☐ _____
_____ ☐ _____
_____ ☐ _____
_____ ☐ _____
_____ ☐ _____

28 TUESDAY

_____ ☐ _____
_____ ☐ _____
_____ ☐ _____
_____ ☐ _____
_____ ☐ _____
_____ ☐ _____
_____ ☐ _____
_____ ☐ _____
_____ ☐ _____
_____ ☐ _____
_____ ☐ _____

29 WEDNESDAY

_____ ☐ _____
_____ ☐ _____
_____ ☐ _____
_____ ☐ _____
_____ ☐ _____
_____ ☐ _____
_____ ☐ _____
_____ ☐ _____
_____ ☐ _____
_____ ☐ _____
_____ ☐ _____

September 2021

30 THURSDAY

☐
☐
☐
☐
☐
☐
☐
☐
☐
☐
☐

1 FRIDAY

☐
☐
☐
☐
☐
☐
☐
☐
☐
☐
☐

2 SATURDAY

3 SUNDAY

October 2021

SUNDAY	MONDAY	TUESDAY	WEDNESDAY
3	4	5	6
10	11 Columbus Day	12	13
17	18	19	20
24	25	26	27
31 Halloween			

True happiness is... to enjoy the present, without anxious dependence upon the future.

– Lucius Annaeus Seneca

THURSDAY	FRIDAY	SATURDAY	NOTES
	1	2	
7	8	9	
14	15	16	
21	22	23	
28	29	30	

October 2021

4 MONDAY

☐
☐
☐
☐
☐
☐
☐
☐
☐
☐
☐

5 TUESDAY

☐
☐
☐
☐
☐
☐
☐
☐
☐
☐
☐

6 WEDNESDAY

☐
☐
☐
☐
☐
☐
☐
☐
☐
☐
☐

7 THURSDAY

☐
☐
☐
☐
☐
☐
☐
☐
☐
☐
☐
☐

8 FRIDAY

☐
☐
☐
☐
☐
☐
☐
☐
☐
☐
☐

9 SATURDAY

10 SUNDAY

October 2021

11 **MONDAY**

Columbus Day

☐
☐
☐
☐
☐
☐
☐
☐
☐
☐
☐

12 **TUESDAY**

☐
☐
☐
☐
☐
☐
☐
☐
☐
☐
☐

13 **WEDNESDAY**

☐
☐
☐
☐
☐
☐
☐
☐
☐
☐
☐

14 THURSDAY

☐
☐
☐
☐
☐
☐
☐
☐
☐
☐
☐

15 FRIDAY

☐
☐
☐
☐
☐
☐
☐
☐
☐
☐
☐

16 SATURDAY

17 SUNDAY

October 2021

18 MONDAY

☐

☐

☐

☐

☐

☐

☐

☐

☐

☐

☐

19 TUESDAY

☐

☐

☐

☐

☐

☐

☐

☐

☐

☐

☐

20 WEDNESDAY

☐

☐

☐

☐

☐

☐

☐

☐

☐

☐

☐

October 2021

21 THURSDAY

- [ ]
- [ ]
- [ ]
- [ ]
- [ ]
- [ ]
- [ ]
- [ ]
- [ ]
- [ ]
- [ ]

22 FRIDAY

- [ ]
- [ ]
- [ ]
- [ ]
- [ ]
- [ ]
- [ ]
- [ ]
- [ ]
- [ ]
- [ ]

23 SATURDAY

24 SUNDAY

October 2021

25 MONDAY

26 TUESDAY

27 WEDNESDAY

28 **THURSDAY**

☐
☐
☐
☐
☐
☐
☐
☐
☐
☐
☐

29 **FRIDAY**

☐
☐
☐
☐
☐
☐
☐
☐
☐
☐
☐
☐

30 **SATURDAY**

31 **SUNDAY**

Halloween

November 2021

SUNDAY	MONDAY	TUESDAY	WEDNESDAY
	1	**2** Election Day	**3**
7 Daylight Saving Time Ends	**8**	**9**	**10**
14	**15**	**16**	**17**
21	**22**	**23**	**24**
28 Hanukkah, Begins at Sunset	**29**	**30**	

Be kind. Every person you meet is fighting a difficult battle.
– Plato

THURSDAY	FRIDAY	SATURDAY	NOTES
4	**5**	**6**	
11 Veterans Day	**12**	**13**	
18	**19**	**20**	
25 Thanksgiving Day	**26**	**27**	

November 2021

1 MONDAY

☐
☐
☐
☐
☐
☐
☐
☐
☐
☐
☐

2 TUESDAY

Election Day

☐
☐
☐
☐
☐
☐
☐
☐
☐
☐
☐

3 WEDNESDAY

☐
☐
☐
☐
☐
☐
☐
☐
☐
☐
☐

4 **THURSDAY**

- [ ]
- [ ]
- [ ]
- [ ]
- [ ]
- [ ]
- [ ]
- [ ]
- [ ]
- [ ]
- [ ]

5 **FRIDAY**

- [ ]
- [ ]
- [ ]
- [ ]
- [ ]
- [ ]
- [ ]
- [ ]
- [ ]
- [ ]
- [ ]

6 **SATURDAY**

7 **SUNDAY**

Daylight Saving Time Ends

November 2021

8 MONDAY

☐
☐
☐
☐
☐
☐
☐
☐
☐
☐
☐

9 TUESDAY

☐
☐
☐
☐
☐
☐
☐
☐
☐
☐
☐

10 WEDNESDAY

☐
☐
☐
☐
☐
☐
☐
☐
☐
☐
☐

November 2021

11 **THURSDAY**

Veterans Day

☐
☐
☐
☐
☐
☐
☐
☐
☐
☐
☐

12 **FRIDAY**

☐
☐
☐
☐
☐
☐
☐
☐
☐
☐
☐

13 **SATURDAY**

14 **SUNDAY**

November 2021

15 MONDAY

☐
☐
☐
☐
☐
☐
☐
☐
☐
☐

16 TUESDAY

☐
☐
☐
☐
☐
☐
☐
☐
☐
☐
☐

17 WEDNESDAY

☐
☐
☐
☐
☐
☐
☐
☐
☐
☐
☐

18 THURSDAY

☐
☐
☐
☐
☐
☐
☐
☐
☐
☐
☐

19 FRIDAY

☐
☐
☐
☐
☐
☐
☐
☐
☐
☐
☐

20 SATURDAY

21 SUNDAY

November 2021

22 MONDAY

☐
☐
☐
☐
☐
☐
☐
☐
☐
☐
☐

23 TUESDAY

☐
☐
☐
☐
☐
☐
☐
☐
☐
☐
☐

24 WEDNESDAY

☐
☐
☐
☐
☐
☐
☐
☐
☐
☐
☐
☐

November 2021

25 **THURSDAY**

Thanksgiving Day

☐
☐
☐
☐
☐
☐
☐
☐
☐
☐
☐

26 **FRIDAY**

☐
☐
☐
☐
☐
☐
☐
☐
☐
☐
☐

27 **SATURDAY**

28 **SUNDAY**

Hanukkah, Begins at Sunset

December 2021

SUNDAY	MONDAY	TUESDAY	WEDNESDAY
			1
5	6	7	8
12	13	14	15
19	20	21 First Day of Winter	22
26 Kwanzaa Begins	27	28	29

Every expert was once a beginner.
– Rutherford B. Hayes

THURSDAY	FRIDAY	SATURDAY	NOTES
2	3	4	
9	10	11	
16	17	18	
23	24	25 Christmas Day	
30	31 New Year's Eve		

November 2021

29 MONDAY

☐
☐
☐
☐
☐
☐
☐
☐
☐
☐
☐

30 TUESDAY

☐
☐
☐
☐
☐
☐
☐
☐
☐
☐
☐

1 WEDNESDAY

☐
☐
☐
☐
☐
☐
☐
☐
☐
☐
☐
☐

December 2021

2 **THURSDAY**

☐
☐
☐
☐
☐
☐
☐
☐
☐
☐
☐

3 **FRIDAY**

☐
☐
☐
☐
☐
☐
☐
☐
☐
☐
☐

4 **SATURDAY**

5 **SUNDAY**

December 2021

6 MONDAY

☐
☐
☐
☐
☐
☐
☐
☐
☐
☐
☐

7 TUESDAY

☐
☐
☐
☐
☐
☐
☐
☐
☐
☐
☐

8 WEDNESDAY

☐
☐
☐
☐
☐
☐
☐
☐
☐
☐
☐

December 2021

9 **THURSDAY**

☐
☐
☐
☐
☐
☐
☐
☐
☐
☐
☐

10 **FRIDAY**

☐
☐
☐
☐
☐
☐
☐
☐
☐
☐
☐

11 **SATURDAY**

12 **SUNDAY**

December 2021

13 MONDAY

- [ ]
- [ ]
- [ ]
- [ ]
- [ ]
- [ ]
- [ ]
- [ ]
- [ ]
- [ ]

14 TUESDAY

- [ ]
- [ ]
- [ ]
- [ ]
- [ ]
- [ ]
- [ ]
- [ ]
- [ ]
- [ ]
- [ ]

15 WEDNESDAY

- [ ]
- [ ]
- [ ]
- [ ]
- [ ]
- [ ]
- [ ]
- [ ]
- [ ]
- [ ]
- [ ]

16 THURSDAY

☐
☐
☐
☐
☐
☐
☐
☐
☐
☐
☐

17 FRIDAY

☐
☐
☐
☐
☐
☐
☐
☐
☐
☐
☐

18 SATURDAY

19 SUNDAY

December 2021

20 **MONDAY**

☐
☐
☐
☐
☐
☐
☐
☐
☐
☐

21 **TUESDAY**

First Day of Winter

☐
☐
☐
☐
☐
☐
☐
☐
☐
☐

22 **WEDNESDAY**

☐
☐
☐
☐
☐
☐
☐
☐
☐
☐

23 THURSDAY

☐
☐
☐
☐
☐
☐
☐
☐
☐
☐
☐

24 FRIDAY

☐
☐
☐
☐
☐
☐
☐
☐
☐
☐
☐

25 SATURDAY

Christmas Day

26 SUNDAY

Kwanzaa Begins

December 2021

27 MONDAY

☐
☐
☐
☐
☐
☐
☐
☐
☐
☐
☐

28 TUESDAY

☐
☐
☐
☐
☐
☐
☐
☐
☐
☐
☐

29 WEDNESDAY

☐
☐
☐
☐
☐
☐
☐
☐
☐
☐

December 2021

30 **THURSDAY**

☐
☐
☐
☐
☐
☐
☐
☐
☐
☐
☐

31 **FRIDAY**

New Year's Eve

☐
☐
☐
☐
☐
☐
☐
☐
☐
☐
☐

1 **SATURDAY**

New Year's Day

2 **SUNDAY**

January 2022

SUNDAY	MONDAY	TUESDAY	WEDNESDAY
2	3	4	5
9	10	11	12
16	17 Martin Luther King, Jr. Day	18	19
23	24	25	26
30	31		

Have more than you show, Speak less than you know.

– William Shakespeare

THURSDAY	FRIDAY	SATURDAY	NOTES
		1 New Year's Day	
6	**7**	**8**	
13	**14**	**15**	
20	**21**	**22**	
27	**28**	**29**	

January 2022

3 **MONDAY**

☐
☐
☐
☐
☐
☐
☐
☐
☐
☐
☐

4 **TUESDAY**

☐
☐
☐
☐
☐
☐
☐
☐
☐
☐
☐

5 **WEDNESDAY**

☐
☐
☐
☐
☐
☐
☐
☐
☐
☐
☐

6 **THURSDAY**

☐
☐
☐
☐
☐
☐
☐
☐
☐
☐
☐

7 **FRIDAY**

☐
☐
☐
☐
☐
☐
☐
☐
☐
☐
☐

8 **SATURDAY**

9 **SUNDAY**

January 2022

10 MONDAY

☐
☐
☐
☐
☐
☐
☐
☐
☐
☐
☐

11 TUESDAY

☐
☐
☐
☐
☐
☐
☐
☐
☐
☐
☐

12 WEDNESDAY

☐
☐
☐
☐
☐
☐
☐
☐
☐
☐
☐

January 2022

13 THURSDAY

☐
☐
☐
☐
☐
☐
☐
☐
☐
☐
☐

14 FRIDAY

☐
☐
☐
☐
☐
☐
☐
☐
☐
☐
☐

15 SATURDAY

16 SUNDAY

January 2022

17 **MONDAY**

Martin Luther King, Jr. Day

☐
☐
☐
☐
☐
☐
☐
☐
☐
☐
☐

18 **TUESDAY**

☐
☐
☐
☐
☐
☐
☐
☐
☐
☐
☐

19 **WEDNESDAY**

☐
☐
☐
☐
☐
☐
☐
☐
☐
☐
☐

January 2022

20 THURSDAY

- [ ]
- [ ]
- [ ]
- [ ]
- [ ]
- [ ]
- [ ]
- [ ]
- [ ]
- [ ]
- [ ]

21 FRIDAY

- [ ]
- [ ]
- [ ]
- [ ]
- [ ]
- [ ]
- [ ]
- [ ]
- [ ]
- [ ]
- [ ]

22 SATURDAY

23 SUNDAY

January 2022

24 MONDAY

☐
☐
☐
☐
☐
☐
☐
☐
☐
☐
☐

25 TUESDAY

☐
☐
☐
☐
☐
☐
☐
☐
☐
☐
☐

26 WEDNESDAY

☐
☐
☐
☐
☐
☐
☐
☐
☐
☐
☐
☐

27 **THURSDAY**

- [ ]
- [ ]
- [ ]
- [ ]
- [ ]
- [ ]
- [ ]
- [ ]
- [ ]
- [ ]
- [ ]

28 **FRIDAY**

- [ ]
- [ ]
- [ ]
- [ ]
- [ ]
- [ ]
- [ ]
- [ ]
- [ ]
- [ ]
- [ ]

29 **SATURDAY**

30 **SUNDAY**

February 2022

SUNDAY	MONDAY	TUESDAY	WEDNESDAY
		1	**2**
6	**7**	**8**	**9**
13	**14** Valentine's Day	**15**	**16**
20	**21** Presidents' Day	**22**	**23**
27	**28**		

Times change, and we change with them.
– William Henry Harrison

THURSDAY	FRIDAY	SATURDAY	NOTES
3	4	5	
10	11	12	
17	18	19	
24	25	26	

January 2022

31 MONDAY

1 TUESDAY

2 WEDNESDAY

February 2022

3 THURSDAY

☐

4 FRIDAY

☐

5 SATURDAY

6 SUNDAY

February 2022

7 **MONDAY**

☐
☐
☐
☐
☐
☐
☐
☐
☐
☐
☐

8 **TUESDAY**

☐
☐
☐
☐
☐
☐
☐
☐
☐
☐
☐

9 **WEDNESDAY**

☐
☐
☐
☐
☐
☐
☐
☐
☐
☐
☐

10 THURSDAY

☐
☐
☐
☐
☐
☐
☐
☐
☐
☐
☐

11 FRIDAY

☐
☐
☐
☐
☐
☐
☐
☐
☐
☐
☐

12 SATURDAY

13 SUNDAY

February 2022

14 MONDAY

Valentine's Day

- [ ]
- [ ]
- [ ]
- [ ]
- [ ]
- [ ]
- [ ]
- [ ]
- [ ]
- [ ]

15 TUESDAY

- [ ]
- [ ]
- [ ]
- [ ]
- [ ]
- [ ]
- [ ]
- [ ]
- [ ]
- [ ]
- [ ]

16 WEDNESDAY

- [ ]
- [ ]
- [ ]
- [ ]
- [ ]
- [ ]
- [ ]
- [ ]
- [ ]
- [ ]

February 2022

17 **THURSDAY**

☐
☐
☐
☐
☐
☐
☐
☐
☐
☐
☐

18 **FRIDAY**

☐
☐
☐
☐
☐
☐
☐
☐
☐
☐
☐

19 **SATURDAY**

20 **SUNDAY**

February 2022

21 **MONDAY**

Presidents' Day

☐
☐
☐
☐
☐
☐
☐
☐
☐
☐
☐

22 **TUESDAY**

☐
☐
☐
☐
☐
☐
☐
☐
☐
☐
☐

23 **WEDNESDAY**

☐
☐
☐
☐
☐
☐
☐
☐
☐
☐
☐

24 THURSDAY

☐
☐
☐
☐
☐
☐
☐
☐
☐
☐
☐
☐

25 FRIDAY

☐
☐
☐
☐
☐
☐
☐
☐
☐
☐
☐

26 SATURDAY

27 SUNDAY

March 2022

SUNDAY	MONDAY	TUESDAY	WEDNESDAY
		1	**2** Ash Wednesday
6	**7**	**8**	**9**
13 Daylight Saving Time Begins	**14**	**15**	**16**
20 First Day of Spring	**21**	**22**	**23**
27	**28**	**29**	**30**

Believe you can and you're halfway there.
– Theodore Roosevelt

THURSDAY	FRIDAY	SATURDAY	NOTES
3	**4**	**5**	
10	**11**	**12**	
17 St. Patrick's Day	**18**	**19**	
24	**25**	**26**	
31			

February 2022

28 MONDAY

☐
☐
☐
☐
☐
☐
☐
☐
☐
☐
☐

1 TUESDAY

☐
☐
☐
☐
☐
☐
☐
☐
☐
☐
☐

2 WEDNESDAY

Ash Wednesday

☐
☐
☐
☐
☐
☐
☐
☐
☐
☐
☐

3 **THURSDAY**

☐
☐
☐
☐
☐
☐
☐
☐
☐
☐
☐

4 **FRIDAY**

☐
☐
☐
☐
☐
☐
☐
☐
☐
☐
☐

5 **SATURDAY**

6 **SUNDAY**

March 2022

7 **MONDAY**

☐
☐
☐
☐
☐
☐
☐
☐
☐
☐
☐

8 **TUESDAY**

☐
☐
☐
☐
☐
☐
☐
☐
☐
☐
☐

9 **WEDNESDAY**

☐
☐
☐
☐
☐
☐
☐
☐
☐
☐
☐

10 **THURSDAY**

☐
☐
☐
☐
☐
☐
☐
☐
☐
☐
☐

11 **FRIDAY**

☐
☐
☐
☐
☐
☐
☐
☐
☐
☐
☐

12 **SATURDAY**

13 **SUNDAY**

Daylight Saving Time Begins

March 2022

14 MONDAY

☐
☐
☐
☐
☐
☐
☐
☐
☐
☐
☐

15 TUESDAY

☐
☐
☐
☐
☐
☐
☐
☐
☐
☐
☐

16 WEDNESDAY

☐
☐
☐
☐
☐
☐
☐
☐
☐
☐
☐

17 THURSDAY

St. Patrick's Day

☐
☐
☐
☐
☐
☐
☐
☐
☐
☐
☐

18 FRIDAY

☐
☐
☐
☐
☐
☐
☐
☐
☐
☐
☐

19 SATURDAY

20 SUNDAY

First Day of Spring

March 2022

21 MONDAY

☐
☐
☐
☐
☐
☐
☐
☐
☐
☐
☐

22 TUESDAY

☐
☐
☐
☐
☐
☐
☐
☐
☐
☐
☐

23 WEDNESDAY

☐
☐
☐
☐
☐
☐
☐
☐
☐
☐
☐
☐

24 THURSDAY

☐
☐
☐
☐
☐
☐
☐
☐
☐
☐
☐

25 FRIDAY

☐
☐
☐
☐
☐
☐
☐
☐
☐
☐
☐

26 SATURDAY

27 SUNDAY

March 2022

28 MONDAY

☐

☐

☐

☐

☐

☐

☐

☐

☐

☐

☐

29 TUESDAY

☐

☐

☐

☐

☐

☐

☐

☐

☐

☐

☐

30 WEDNESDAY

☐

☐

☐

☐

☐

☐

☐

☐

☐

☐

☐

☐

March 2022

31 THURSDAY

☐
☐
☐
☐
☐
☐
☐
☐
☐
☐
☐

1 FRIDAY

☐
☐
☐
☐
☐
☐
☐
☐
☐
☐
☐

2 SATURDAY

3 SUNDAY

April 2022

SUNDAY	MONDAY	TUESDAY	WEDNESDAY
3	**4**	**5**	**6**
10 Palm Sunday	**11**	**12**	**13**
17 Easter	**18**	**19**	**20**
24	**25**	**26**	**27**

To be good, and to do good, is all we have to do.

– John Adams

THURSDAY	FRIDAY	SATURDAY	NOTES
	1	**2**	
7	**8**	**9**	
14	**15** Good Friday Passover, Begins at Sunset	**16**	
21	**22** Earth Day	**23**	
28	**29**	**30**	

April 2022

4 MONTH

☐
☐
☐
☐
☐
☐
☐
☐
☐
☐
☐

5 TUESDAY

☐
☐
☐
☐
☐
☐
☐
☐
☐
☐
☐

6 WEDNESDAY

☐
☐
☐
☐
☐
☐
☐
☐
☐
☐
☐

7 **THURSDAY**

8 **FRIDAY**

9 **SATURDAY**

10 **SUNDAY**

Palm Sunday

April 2022

11 MONDAY

☐
☐
☐
☐
☐
☐
☐
☐
☐
☐
☐

12 TUESDAY

☐
☐
☐
☐
☐
☐
☐
☐
☐
☐
☐

13 WEDNESDAY

☐
☐
☐
☐
☐
☐
☐
☐
☐
☐
☐

April 2022

14 THURSDAY

- [ ]
- [ ]
- [ ]
- [ ]
- [ ]
- [ ]
- [ ]
- [ ]
- [ ]
- [ ]
- [ ]

15 FRIDAY

Good Friday

Passover, Begins at Sunset

- [ ]
- [ ]
- [ ]
- [ ]
- [ ]
- [ ]
- [ ]
- [ ]
- [ ]
- [ ]
- [ ]

16 SATURDAY

17 SUNDAY

Easter

April 2022

18 MONDAY

19 TUESDAY

20 WEDNESDAY

21 **THURSDAY**

☐
☐
☐
☐
☐
☐
☐
☐
☐
☐
☐

22 **FRIDAY**

Earth Day

☐
☐
☐
☐
☐
☐
☐
☐
☐
☐
☐

23 **SATURDAY**

24 **SUNDAY**

April 2022

25 MONDAY

☐
☐
☐
☐
☐
☐
☐
☐
☐
☐
☐

26 TUESDAY

☐
☐
☐
☐
☐
☐
☐
☐
☐
☐
☐

27 WEDNESDAY

☐
☐
☐
☐
☐
☐
☐
☐
☐
☐
☐

April 2022

28 THURSDAY

☐
☐
☐
☐
☐
☐
☐
☐
☐
☐
☐

29 FRIDAY

☐
☐
☐
☐
☐
☐
☐
☐
☐
☐
☐

30 SATURDAY

1 SUNDAY

May 2022

SUNDAY	MONDAY	TUESDAY	WEDNESDAY
1	2	3	4
8 Mother's Day	9	10	11
15	16	17	18
22	23	24	25
29	30 Memorial Day	31	

Do you want to know who you are? Don't ask. Act! Action will delineate and define you.

– Thomas Jefferson

THURSDAY	FRIDAY	SATURDAY	NOTES
5	6	7	
12	13	14	
19	20	21	
26	27	28	

May 2022

2 **MONDAY**

☐
☐
☐
☐
☐
☐
☐
☐
☐
☐
☐

3 **TUESDAY**

☐
☐
☐
☐
☐
☐
☐
☐
☐
☐
☐

4 **WEDNESDAY**

☐
☐
☐
☐
☐
☐
☐
☐
☐
☐
☐

May 2022

5 THURSDAY

- [ ]
- [ ]
- [ ]
- [ ]
- [ ]
- [ ]
- [ ]
- [ ]
- [ ]
- [ ]
- [ ]

6 FRIDAY

- [ ]
- [ ]
- [ ]
- [ ]
- [ ]
- [ ]
- [ ]
- [ ]
- [ ]
- [ ]
- [ ]

7 SATURDAY

8 SUNDAY

Mother's Day

May 2022

9 MONDAY

10 TUESDAY

11 WEDNESDAY

12 THURSDAY

☐
☐
☐
☐
☐
☐
☐
☐
☐
☐
☐

13 FRIDAY

☐
☐
☐
☐
☐
☐
☐
☐
☐
☐
☐

14 SATURDAY

15 SUNDAY

May 2022

16 **MONDAY**

☐
☐
☐
☐
☐
☐
☐
☐
☐
☐
☐

17 **TUESDAY**

☐
☐
☐
☐
☐
☐
☐
☐
☐
☐
☐

18 **WEDNESDAY**

☐
☐
☐
☐
☐
☐
☐
☐
☐
☐
☐

19 THURSDAY

☐
☐
☐
☐
☐
☐
☐
☐
☐
☐
☐
☐

20 FRIDAY

☐
☐
☐
☐
☐
☐
☐
☐
☐
☐
☐

21 SATURDAY

22 SUNDAY

May 2022

23 MONDAY

24 TUESDAY

25 WEDNESDAY

May 2022

26 THURSDAY

☐
☐
☐
☐
☐
☐
☐
☐
☐
☐
☐

27 FRIDAY

☐
☐
☐
☐
☐
☐
☐
☐
☐
☐
☐

28 SATURDAY

29 SUNDAY

June 2022

SUNDAY	MONDAY	TUESDAY	WEDNESDAY
			1
5	**6**	**7**	**8**
12	**13**	**14** Flag Day	**15**
19 Father's Day	**20**	**21** First Day of Summer	**22**
26	**27**	**28**	**29**

The greatest danger for most of us is not that our aim is too high and we miss it, but that it is too low and we reach it.

– Michaelangelo

THURSDAY	FRIDAY	SATURDAY	NOTES
2	3	4	
9	10	11	
16	17	18	
23	24	25	
30			

May 2022

30 **MONDAY**

Memorial Day

☐
☐
☐
☐
☐
☐
☐
☐
☐
☐
☐

31 **TUESDAY**

☐
☐
☐
☐
☐
☐
☐
☐
☐
☐
☐

1 **WEDNESDAY**

☐
☐
☐
☐
☐
☐
☐
☐
☐
☐
☐

2 **THURSDAY**

☐
☐
☐
☐
☐
☐
☐
☐
☐
☐
☐

3 **FRIDAY**

☐
☐
☐
☐
☐
☐
☐
☐
☐
☐
☐

4 **SATURDAY**

5 **SUNDAY**

June 2022

6 **MONDAY**

_____

☐
☐
☐
☐
☐
☐
☐
☐
☐
☐
☐

7 **TUESDAY**

_____

☐
☐
☐
☐
☐
☐
☐
☐
☐
☐
☐

8 **WEDNESDAY**

_____

☐
☐
☐
☐
☐
☐
☐
☐
☐
☐
☐

9 THURSDAY

☐
☐
☐
☐
☐
☐
☐
☐
☐
☐
☐
☐

10 FRIDAY

☐
☐
☐
☐
☐
☐
☐
☐
☐
☐
☐

11 SATURDAY

12 SUNDAY

June 2022

13 **MONDAY**

- ☐
- ☐
- ☐
- ☐
- ☐
- ☐
- ☐
- ☐
- ☐
- ☐
- ☐

14 **TUESDAY**

Flag Day

- ☐
- ☐
- ☐
- ☐
- ☐
- ☐
- ☐
- ☐
- ☐
- ☐
- ☐

15 **WEDNESDAY**

- ☐
- ☐
- ☐
- ☐
- ☐
- ☐
- ☐
- ☐
- ☐
- ☐
- ☐

16 THURSDAY

☐
☐
☐
☐
☐
☐
☐
☐
☐
☐
☐

17 FRIDAY

☐
☐
☐
☐
☐
☐
☐
☐
☐
☐
☐

18 SATURDAY

19 SUNDAY

Father's Day

June 2022

20 **MONDAY**

_____

☐ _____
☐ _____
☐ _____
☐ _____
☐ _____
☐ _____
☐ _____
☐ _____
☐ _____
☐ _____
☐ _____

21 **TUESDAY**

First Day of Summer

_____

☐ _____
☐ _____
☐ _____
☐ _____
☐ _____
☐ _____
☐ _____
☐ _____
☐ _____
☐ _____
☐ _____

22 **WEDNESDAY**

_____

☐ _____
☐ _____
☐ _____
☐ _____
☐ _____
☐ _____
☐ _____
☐ _____
☐ _____
☐ _____
☐ _____

23 THURSDAY

☐
☐
☐
☐
☐
☐
☐
☐
☐
☐
☐

24 FRIDAY

☐
☐
☐
☐
☐
☐
☐
☐
☐
☐
☐

25 SATURDAY

26 SUNDAY

June 2022

27 MONDAY

☐
☐
☐
☐
☐
☐
☐
☐
☐
☐
☐
☐

28 TUESDAY

☐
☐
☐
☐
☐
☐
☐
☐
☐
☐
☐

29 WEDNESDAY

☐
☐
☐
☐
☐
☐
☐
☐
☐
☐
☐

June 2022

30 **THURSDAY**

☐
☐
☐
☐
☐
☐
☐
☐
☐
☐
☐

1 **FRIDAY**

☐
☐
☐
☐
☐
☐
☐
☐
☐
☐
☐

2 **SATURDAY**

3 **SUNDAY**

2022

JANUARY

SUN	MON	TUE	WED	THU	FRI	SAT
						1
2	3	4	5	6	7	8
9	10	11	12	13	14	15
16	17	18	19	20	21	22
23	24	25	26	27	28	29
30	31					

FEBRUARY

SUN	MON	TUE	WED	THU	FRI	SAT
		1	2	3	4	5
6	7	8	9	10	11	12
13	14	15	16	17	18	19
20	21	22	23	24	25	26
27	28					

MARCH

SUN	MON	TUE	WED	THU	FRI	SAT
		1	2	3	4	5
6	7	8	9	10	11	12
13	14	15	16	17	18	19
20	21	22	23	24	25	26
27	28	29	30	31		

APRIL

SUN	MON	TUE	WED	THU	FRI	SAT
					1	2
3	4	5	6	7	8	9
10	11	12	13	14	15	16
17	18	19	20	21	22	23
24	25	26	27	28	29	30

MAY

SUN	MON	TUE	WED	THU	FRI	SAT
1	2	3	4	5	6	7
8	9	10	11	12	13	14
15	16	17	18	19	20	21
22	23	24	25	26	27	28
29	30	31				

JUNE

SUN	MON	TUE	WED	THU	FRI	SAT
			1	2	3	4
5	6	7	8	9	10	11
12	13	14	15	16	17	18
19	20	21	22	23	24	25
26	27	28	29	30		

JULY

SUN	MON	TUE	WED	THU	FRI	SAT
					1	2
3	4	5	6	7	8	9
10	11	12	13	14	15	16
17	18	19	20	21	22	23
24	25	26	27	28	29	30
31						

AUGUST

SUN	MON	TUE	WED	THU	FRI	SAT
	1	2	3	4	5	6
7	8	9	10	11	12	13
14	15	16	17	18	19	20
21	22	23	24	25	26	27
28	29	30	31			

SEPTEMBER

SUN	MON	TUE	WED	THU	FRI	SAT
				1	2	3
4	5	6	7	8	9	10
11	12	13	14	15	16	17
18	19	20	21	22	23	24
25	26	27	28	29	30	

OCTOBER

SUN	MON	TUE	WED	THU	FRI	SAT
						1
2	3	4	5	6	7	8
9	10	11	12	13	14	15
16	17	18	19	20	21	22
23	24	25	26	27	28	29
30	31					

NOVEMBER

SUN	MON	TUE	WED	THU	FRI	SAT
		1	2	3	4	5
6	7	8	9	10	11	12
13	14	15	16	17	18	19
20	21	22	23	24	25	26
27	28	29	30			

DECEMBER

SUN	MON	TUE	WED	THU	FRI	SAT
				1	2	3
4	5	6	7	8	9	10
11	12	13	14	15	16	17
18	19	20	21	22	23	24
25	26	27	28	29	30	31

NOTES

NOTES